MILLIE COLLINS, YOUR BARN IS GONE

by Sherri Felt Dratfield

Červená Barva Press
Somerville, Massachusetts

Červená Barva Press
P.O. Box 440357
W. Somerville, MA 02144-3222

www.cervenabarvapress.com
Bookstore: www.thelostbookshelf.com

Cover art: *Hoosick Falls Barn* monotype by Mary Beth McKenzie
    www.marybethmckenzie.com

Cover Design: William J. Kelle
Production: Steve Asmussen

ISBN: 978-1-950063-07-9

Library of Congress Control Number: 2020936325

CONTENTS

MILLIE COLLINS, YOUR BARN IS GONE

Acknowledgments

The author gratefully acknowledges the publishers of the publications listed below, in which the following poems previously appeared, some in prior versions:

Finishing Line Press – publisher of chapbook Water Vigils (2014 Pushcart nomination)

    Divine Egg

    The Breezes

    Wanting

    Peeling Black

    This Roiling Sea

    Jessica Heather Has Run Aground

    A Cappella

    Landbound

    New Boards

Finishing Line Press – publisher of chapbook The City (2013 Pushcart nomination)

    Time Pieces Repaired

    Caffe Reggio Reserved

    Hallelu

Jewish Currents – publisher of Blue Thread Anthology, May 1, 2014

    Hallelu (selected by Joan Larkin as a Finalist in the 2014 Jewish Currents' Raynes Poetry Competition)

Winning Writers – (http://www.winningwriters.com/contests/margaret/2011/ma11_pastwinners.php)

> Time Pieces Repaired (2011 Margaret Reid Prize for Traditional Verse (sestina variation))

Passager – 2017 Poetry Contest Edition

> Up

Truck – (http://halvard-johnson.blogspot.com/2015/01/), January 2015

> Rip Current

Levure Litteraire – Volume 10; (http://levurelitteraire.com/), November 2014

> Spring Tide
> Millie Collins, Your Barn Is Gone
> I Need a Little Bucket
> Peeling Black
> Ellen B. Has Died Alone
> The Star of David

Fulcrum - 2016

> The Sun in Its Jewel Case
> Dear Mary
> Madame Afghanistan

In loving memory of
Syril and Herbert Dratfield, z"l

Chapter 1: an appointed season; an appointed time.

DIVINE EGG

This divinity has no appendages;
It will never walk away from me,
thumb its nose,
strike me down.
It will not turn me into salt.

It poaches gently in a zephyr simmer.
It scrambles like tumbleweed in Spring.
Its sunny side gazes
patiently.
It whips to white peaks.

The egg cannot be everywhere
so we glimpse its color
where ever we are,
for example, the shore:
in the skirts of a wave,
broken, empty sea shells,
sand under bare feet.

The egg's eternal curves:
the pregnant belly the Buddha belly
soft-boiled in a cup the open
mouth the blown bubble the earth
the stone I placed on my mother's grave
yesterday my daughter's head
in the moment of her birth
each tear shed when I die
the aduki bean.

The egg's shell comforts:
no sharp edges,
no beginning,
no end Within

the egg:
new life.

SPRING TIDE

A woman stands on a dune, orange vested.
Her eyes, green, command the sea, will it to stay calm.
Her wavy, sand-colored strands sway in synch with a harmless breeze.
Her heart beats with a rhythmic shoreline that has already forgotten
the ruin left in the wake of its recent
outburst.

The woman stands among a swarm of men in neon-yellow jackets.
They drill holes -
poking in pollen.
She nestles in dune brush,
leans like the patches of tall sea-grass surrounding
her. They are survivors of past storms.

The dune grassers
drill, hum, plant sticks in
slim cavities, dry but willing
to receive these straw bits -
will moisture come,
will roots dig in before more hurricanes arrive?

She bends and plants
on a barren crest,
bends and plants
small stalks,
bends and plants,
bends, plants.

The beach reclaimed, giant pipes are stacked.
The ocean revs, drowns out tractor growls;

the elephantine CAT army scoops up each rusty trunk
to lead the way, bob, sway,
mount, then cross the boardwalk bridge.
Soon all traces of beach-fill machinery will be

gone
to the next site,
down coast.
The woman removes her vest.
She darts a look at the
unrepentant sea.

Rip Current

A man in orange trunks ducks under high breakers,
far from the lifeguard stands,
in the rip-tide sea.

The boat reaches the now vanished orange thread.
The man - retrieved,

plopped on sand like a noonday catch,
(mouth-to-mouth, chest thumping arms) -

is dead.
I have learned to swim across the current grabbing me;

I don't lash opposite the thrusts, against the under tow.
As though it were a beloved in a sudden mood –

bullheaded, dogged – I match the current stroke for stroke,
kick across its belly, until it tires of my moxie.

The sandpiper wears its white feather noose when grown,
is not strangled.

The seagull gobbles a plastic bag as hungrily as crab,
then scavenges a straw.

The duck quacks for more bread,
although, before dawn, a cat

caught the last of her eight ducklings.
Lifeguards keep watch
till Summer's end.

2 O'CLOCK BELLS

I was watching the Campanile when
it happened, seeing bricks topped by
three bells inside three arches;
above the tower, a brick cone.

They rang twice,
three bells in unison.
I saw sound and felt life echo -
brief, gone.

Gargoyle at Chiesa Santa Maria Della Formosa

In front of a wooden door,
gazes lock on a bizarre sight above.
No one notices this squat door
with two outsize keyholes
that have been waiting
centuries to be filled.
The big bronze keys
that never come may hide
just inside the passageway.

Couples pose under the slack-jawed dwarf,
teeth bucked, heavy tongue pressing
down his lip. His right eye looks ever up,
away, avoids the fawning couples.
His left eye is bulbous, closed,
grotesque. His nose skews right.
Tourists adore this misshapen celebrity.
They giggle, take selfies,
wait for their turn, block the door.

LATE IN NEW ORLEANS AT SNUG HARBOR

When I was small in your blue room, Nana,
Durante taught me *the steps*
with top hat and cane that Jackson
(was he dead?) had danced with him.

Won't You Come Home, Bill Bailey?

He made me laugh, the hat so big but
hadda put it on   so   I could take it off.

He kissed me with his nose.

I cried the whole night lo-ong.

He made me work.
He made me like my
skinny   legs.
Soft shoe   us two.

I sang   I waved a cane   tap tap twirl tap

with this new old tickly man,

who made me get it right
and treated me grown-up.

Were you watching, Nana?
You rarely noticed me.
I can't recall your laugh

but your visitor
he is in my heart's harbor,
a close up wrinkly grin.

I know I'm to blame.   Gone,

the vaudeville riff
played by these jazz men.

...now ain't it a shame?

MILLIE COLLINS, YOUR BARN IS GONE

Obbie cleared it after folks
on our road said outright
kids would get hurt.
The floor'd been mostly missing
since just before you died
and took your DAR roots to the grave,
not to mention that poor
nameless mongrel you kept staked
in the front yard.
Never saw him fed or taken in.
Never told you I tossed him bones from the car.

Ob's a fixer but once the roof sagged
that barn was done.
He and Brenda bought your place
from the gal who'd taken care of you
(can't think her name)
those last years. Only good thing
may be you ever did, Millie,
leaving your place to that good woman.

This week, Obbie put a big red barn
just where yours was. Just where.
I watched the whole time Ob was at it. Odd
to see newness on the spot
where, so long ago, you and I
went late one night,
after drinking your cheap tea from chipped cups,
and dug that tiny grave,
deep enough.

*Chapter 2: a time to give birth, to die;
to plant, to uproot.*

ON A BEACH

for this moment, all converge
at shore's edge.

Morning bathers -
splashed children,
dunked lovers,
hand-held elders –
leave off their frolics.

Young ones, all sizes,
form a wedge, crescent-shaped,
to ward off gulls. Specks of sand
from its trek wash off
the tiny shell scrambling into water.

We meet it and, like Nashon,
we wade from shallow
to the deep
with the newborn sea turtle.
It dives, resurfaces, swims beyond.

The followers linger
before we scatter,
turn to umbrellas
with sun beds
all lined up.

Here, where Greek is spoken,
the sand does not yet scorch,
does not yet burn away
our quiet revel, this witness.

ARBOREAL

after "Behind the Mirror", 1937, Oil and sand on canvas, by Rita Kernn-Larsen

It has been years
since I wore high heels. On a raked
stage, I had danced without thought
in shoes, needle-thin
and breathtakingly aloft -
me and my stilettos.

Now, I venture through
the looking glass, perplexed as others
who have awakened on the
precipice of Alice's rabbit hole
with our shoes on.
We have a choice.

We descend together,
the azure staircase and I,
naked, shoeless. In a moment I am
seed, a tree, then redwood trunk with
ages, ages of wisdom, belly stretched
from past births and beckoning

more, despite my age. What will
the children think? As I squirm,
my roots burrow deeper ever deeper
into a looking glass soul. In
easily furrowed soil, I dig in, decided,
but frightened of my new home.

16

Dear Mary

after Frari Triptych, Madonna & Child by Giovanni Bellini, 1488.
Tempura on panel. S. Maria dei Frari, Sacristy, Venice, Italy

With heavy lids, did your eyes dart away
and strain against a blood-stained second sight,
flick back dark thoughts from your son's straw birthright,
unfeel his heartbeats where your fingers lay?

Did you sit still, inhale his baby scent,
enfold his fleshy ribs you loved too much
(those fleeting moments of a mother's touch),
and sense a creeping dread that won't relent?

Did you turn giddy, too, at your son's birth,
then, when menaced by those in royal blue,
dismiss the sacrifice you saw, felt, knew:
slain son; strangling sobs; dark puddles; dank earth?

Your chest, like mine, heaved in surrendered breath.
Tell me, will my boy be spared early death?

Last Grain

Grandpa was old. Susan was seven.
She lived on the beach, two doors down
from his grand house. The desultory sun played
hopscotch every day, or not, on the waves as she ran,
arms flapping, and kicked sand to his house.
The sun sprayed his glass room,
cast shadows.
Each day
the same:
Please can we play? Now,
in your sunny room? Oh, come on,
Grandpa. She tugged his hands, pulled him in.

Grandpa was a collector.
The sunroom was an hourglass play land,
from midget sterling minute timers, to tripod
monoliths spanning five across to measure the sea-hours;
of stone, glint obsidian, red paint, brass, wood, wood on wood,
pewter, copper and, Susan's favorite, antique
with a round green marble
base - color of her eyes
and Grandpa's - and
many shapes,
many sizes.
Most, not
all, had
sand
to
slip
through.
Some had
pulverized
eggshell, but
Susan liked the sand:
just like her beach, but
orange, black and salt-white, too.
She watched them funnel through
and through until the last bit of sand passed.

Grandpa, why do you
collect hourglasses?
Because time is the
one thing we
all have in
common.
When
time
runs
out
we
are
done.
There is
as much
sand as the
hourglass holds

.

ENDIVE

doesn't taste as expected.
The leaves, paunchy and succulent,
shout "celery"
but licorice anise wallops your buds.

Add oil and mustard and there
is a meal. I feel that way about you.
Don't take offense. Vegetables
are basic life. You are, basically, my life.

Basic life is dear to me.
Our garden is for flowers, bushes.
Yes, we have lilacs and roses,
but no edibles. Perhaps

the squirrel who ate our first tomato
17 years ago dissuaded us.
We watched each day for green
to turn red. The squirrel bit quicker.

You surprised me this morning.
You said, *come outside. Look:*
blooming azalea, lilac, marigold and
a tomato plant. We try again.

Autumn Leaving

Murano leaves mark the death of warmth.

Red buries green and no one minds
the wind frosting what was new.

The leaving rustles the quarter-hour bells,
soothes like a rake combing ground.

One felled yellow leaf covers the glimpse
of summer soil where love grew.

Only now can I recount,
in the orange crunch of footfall,

how well we loved and how love's leaving
pined the end of bloom.

Chapter 3: a time to kill, to heal;
to break, to build.

MARA'S ANGEL

side chapel, Chiesa S. Maria di Nazareth, Venice, Italy

Among the six
angels in this chapel,
you chose him.
No other wages war
or grasps a spear, long gone,
stands booted
on his conquered human prey.
His right hand dangles chains
that leash an anguished slave.

It was his face
you loved at first sight:
chiseled features -
smooth, calm -
surrendered to his plight
of vigilance, always.
Long locks pillow his resolve.

You have grown a rope of red hair
to strangle manic demons prowling you.
We rest together in a pew and,
like this archangel, you
fool me with your
stillness, angelic grace.

Noah

He was righteous in his time,
a wretched time of pocked souls.

In a righteous time, would he have been?
He stood stalwart

and did small things that grew.
He heard the Call.

He built a boat,
took wood and made the Ark.

He took beasts.
He sailed.

He saved the small, the large, the two,
the world.

I savor quail;
did he bring two?

And you, my Noah, namesake,
forge paths in corrupt times,

bewildering your high school friends
who wonder what's beneath your robes.

I extol your calls to prayer,
as you sail

against our broken world.

Rain Date

We have this in common,
my friends and me: we broke our arms.
One tripped last week
on a tyke on a tricycle in Riverside Park
and fractured his elbow.
Another fell off her bike last night
at the top of her driveway,
same day she returned from a 250 mile ride,
splintered her wrist.

I broke my elbow,
9 years old,
when my bike fell on top of me
in the ditch where I slipped.
I broke my right wrist twice, too.

No conducting opera or playing piano
for a bit, dear friend.
No bike riding, kayaking, action-trip to Matchu Pichu
for another.
My Brownie beanie days were over with the elbow, not much else.

Nothing goes as planned, so rain dates
give us hope our lives will
not be much disrupted,
that fireworks will wow us,
a day late if need be,
our neighbor's firecrackers will
keep us awake (to think like this)
and two terriers,

frightened but trustworthy, will
bark to keep us safe.
With Alan gone so young,
his widow sits,
shocked, flanked
by their
two sons.
They wear sunglasses inside, except
when wiping eyes.
Eulogies abound:
One son looks like Alan's twin
and resurrects my friend,

but the basso voice dissolves
my fantasy. Laughter erupts,
Alan's humor seduces us again.
The son pretends
(with his stubborn use of present tense)
death is just mirage.

I will call the widow each week -
it is in my calendar,
if I am here.
I pray, head bowed, for a rain date.

I Need a Little Bucket

to collect the sand.
I need a yellow shovel
to dig a moat and
watch the sea fill in.
This is how you make it:
get water in your bucket,
scoop sand in,
make a goo, take a fistful,
slip it through
your fingers,
build a sand castle.
If you have time,
keep dripping,
drip it to the sky.
Gulls will soar above,
then stab a crab -
or your peanut butter sandwich
if you don't watch out.

I need a little bucket
to collect my thoughts,
a shovel to bury my
friend and wonder
if he made the earth that rocky
so he could laugh at
how hard it was
to scoop it on his box until
the hole was filled.

We planted a hibiscus bush
earlier today.
Yes, dug a hole with a shovel,
this time sandy soil,
filled it with this living thing.

The tide is coming in,
washing castles
out to sea.
I run to catch
my shovel,
save it from the sea,
hold it close to me.

ON THE LIDO

The bridge is broken.
An arc, this bridge led the bathers to the sea.
I preferred the direct route, feet through sand.
I preferred the palm tree, stunted though it was,
to the crescent, looming in white steel.
It will be fixed; they've cleared broken parts.

We keep vigil before she departs.
Her breath is broken.
Each time - count 20 of no breath, steel
ourselves each time for more counting. Each time – see?
She gasps, breathes, grips a hand, grasps onto what was.
The tide takes every castle of sand.

Broken shells under foot, buried in sand,
remain. Without pulp of life, these parts
persist. They buoy steps; they speak in crunch. (What was
transforms, still broken.)
They gird us for our own path toward the sea.
Look: cars made of shells in sand, not steel.

She was called *Of Valor*, he *Of Steel*.
They chose the trees and hills, rich soil, not sand.
He said I hate the shore; she missed the sea.
Where is the steel? Today, all the parts
gone, I trace broken
pieces in my mind, rebuild the bridge that was.

Mom's quartz lamp, their new wine glass, his heart - each was
whole, broke. I carry shards with me, steal

glimpses (blurred, broken
snap shots) of what was. Particles of sand,
moistened, dripped, create a castle. Parts
merge. I watch children splashing in the sea.

With both gone, I grapple with the sea.
Why is it calm, lulling? His last breath sound was
a wave lapping shore. It departs
silently, this wave's end. No more steel.
I was wrong. It will not be fixed. Just sand.
Nothing is broken.

The sun departs, crouches in clouds. The sea
rises, rages, swallows the sand, submerges steel.
The bridge was broken.

Chapter 4: a time to weep, to laugh; to wail, to dance.

Pink Tears

There should be bells.

Berliner Dom looms:
massive trident domes,
eclipsed by
one

annihilating dome,
silent as death,
flanked on all sides
by soul-cracked
angels.

Linden trees
blossom,
shed their
pink
tears

below.

Up

You said I was too small
to cross the street myself;
you said you had to look right and left.
There you were, across the street
from me,
sitting on the stoop with Mrs. Peterson.
I was already three
so walked right up to that curb,
looked right and crossed.
The car came from the left and
I thought these exact words, as I sailed in the air
over Carnegie Avenue, Plainfield, New Jersey:
remember this because
this is probably the only double-backward-somersault-in-the-air
you will ever do.

There you were,
bent over me, face squished,
your halo of hair almost
brushing my cheek,
tears on yours. I said *Don't cry, Mommy,*
I'm okay.
You didn't seem mad at me
for crossing, for not looking left,
for making you cross the street to me.

I did not think about the snowbank that
caught me, the pink
snow jacket, fluffy, with its snug hood
cushioning my head. I did not

wonder why you left my tiny self,
unattended,
on the other side of
traffic-ridden Carnegie Avenue,
to chat.
I remember flying, my first,
maybe best, memory.

Teruah

a wailing sound, broken into many parts, heard from the Shofar on Rosh Hashanah.

Your mirror broke.
I wrapped it
in my blanket
to be carted away.
Days later,
my glasses broke.
That evening,
your juice glass,
filled with coffee, ice,
crashed on concrete.
Your spare shot glass
broke, too:
loveseat, carpet, table
shimmered with glass shards.
I thought, tomorrow
I will bring you
coffee ice cream.

Next day,
at 13:47,
in the parking lot
near the baseball field
where our friends
had left their car,
a foul ball
bashed
their windshield,
as Doctor Grim (true) declared you dead,
while I wept,
while I held your soft hand,

while your warmth ebbed,
while I kissed your cheek,
while I whispered
Mom Mom Mom
by your ear,
while I heard
a heart smash,
while I whisked the fly
by your face.

MOTHER

1.

Perhaps it was Death's top hat
flung onto your brow's hook
that cast coal shadows
under your eyes.

Death knew
you loathed the ground,
pulled you to it like a twin,
tilled your skin to ready you,

did a soft-shoe on your chest,
leaned its cane against
your lower back
and shoved.

2.

I did not place you in
gleaming mahogany,
reflecting the bowed heads
of your pallbearers.

No buffed or beveled edges
that invited touching.
No jewel box.

Just plain pine.

The Bells

Dogs.
Gulls
pecking at the garbage.
Sparrows, crumb-starved, pierce hearts with their pin eyes.
No one listens to the bells.
The kids cross Campo Santa Margherita.
The gulls moan
and the sparrows won't give up.
No one hears the bells.
I catch some phrases: *sinistra....*
Un po fredo....buon giorno.
There are clouds.
No one listens as bells toll.
Who knows where I will go today?
I toss a sparrow crumbs;
they all show up, impatient with me now.
I am enthralled by bells no one stops to hear,
the quarter-hour bells
knelling your death.

Dark Space

The empty chair in sun
obscures the dark space
you have left. It followed me
here, sits with me
in *caffès* and I think,
on my journey home,
it will shadow me again.
Eight months ago,
it was a boulder taller
than I and wider than
hope. Tears and time
whittled it to this and,
truthfully, I relish the shade;
I want, if not the weight of you -
which was always slight -
to be draped in
your black shawl. I dread
a time when you
have shrunk
to handkerchief size
and I must recall you
in my pocket,
lift you out
to wipe a tear.

This

She sets down her cello,
he his huskie pup.

They drink their tea
as they have done before
in the tea house garden.

The Carmeni bells pound,
stomping out Japanese strains until,
exhausted, the remaining bell gives way.

Three pigeons light but prefer
the sill next door. Sparrows
swirl and treat with melodic threads.

The pup has not yet learned,
as these lovers have, to sit, just watch
while lapping tea.

He nips at hands,
tugs his leash,
upends a chair.

They laugh, trading tranquility
for this.

Length of Days*

The Weavers.
After the hummingbird film,
we watched one on the Weavers,
those singing labor activists with tunes to right most wrongs -
Pete's chin jutting to heaven as he strummed his banjo,
Ronnie's lilt as pert as she no matter what she sang.
That touched my heart.
Herb, just home from rehab,
has an extra beat they found this time around.
For each minute at rest,
there are 600 beats of a hummingbird's heart.
Pete Seeger and Lee Hays wrote songs most folks know,
like *If I had a Hammer.* Seismic years.
The Weavers were blacklisted by McCarthy
but weren't commies. Herb was,
and hid from him in Newark.
On Pier 40, Pete sang *Abiyoyo* to Herb's grandson
when he was two, straddling Simon's shoulders.
Lee Hays died at 90,
ashes mixed in his compost pile.
30 years ago.

Hummingbirds.
Wings flap in figure eights for faster darting
and for hovering
and for flying backwards.
Nests, no bigger than walnuts,
hold two eggs, tic-tac sized.
Beaks are fitted to their flowers -
some hooked,

some longer than the birds themselves
to get the nectar tucked at the top of
giant trumpet blossoms.
Herb, well, we flowers fit ourselves to him.
There's nectar, just the same.
Hummingbirds can live 12 years.
Seems a long time when butterflies
die in a day.

Madagascar.
In Madagascar,
shy spiny lizards grow to 22 inches,
so says the strange birthday card.
Herb is 5' 6" and turned 89 today -
first day of Spring. It snowed.
My Mom stood 5' on her tallest days.
The smallest of warm blooded creatures:
the hummingbird.
One Madagascar tribe buries its dead
and years later, digs them up,
dusts them off,
douses them with wine,
hoists those beloved bones
and they dance all night.
Brass bands belt melodies and everyone,
alive or dead,
is drunk.

Dancing With the Dead.
The endangered Marvelous Spatuletail
twirls two fan-like balls,
a dance, at the end of his tail.
Not the ballroom dance I watched
as Mom and Dad grasped, sashayed and twirled.
In a celebratory trot,
years from now,
when the ache of her loss subsides,
I will sprinkle her bones with Tattinger.
Will she ride astride my shoulders then
as I ride on hers now?
Herb says to mix a tool or two
and 40's photos with his ashes,
like the one from the Robeson Peekskill concert
when Herb was part of the human wall.
But today,
Herb's heart skips a beat.
His gray eyes still dance.

*inspired by "Hummingbirds, Magic in the Air", PBS Nature Program,
Episode first aired 1/10/10*

Chapter 5: a time to cast stones, to gather stones; to embrace, to refrain from embracing.

SANTORINI

A vessel approaches the caldera.
Its sudden swerve creates a half-moon wake.
The twin sails, black, retreat
from oncoming sunset.

The globe, bloodied, dying,
sinks below crags of basalt,
scattered stones, ash,
into its watery
coffin, watched
by vacationing eyes.

Enthralled by this dramatic
departure, the sips, the chewing,
swallows
stop.
See the last claw of sun
submerge, as

one hawk hovers
unvexed by winds,
unmoved by setting sun,
glides
on singular currents.
We resume.
Some will hear the hawk's refrain:
resume resume;
I hear:
resurrection comes each morning.

TREASURE

"I find letters from God, dropt in the street,…" —*Walt Whitman*

First a dime, then a penny, another penny,
gritty bits on the street, the pavement,
on my way to you. 12 cents.

I picked them up, of course,
metal crumbs leading me down the path.

Many pass by,
too rushed, unimpressed,
or disgusted by where they lay

to stoop and scoop up these tiny chips. I know
God left them for me

to deposit – these talismans of good fortune,
hope – in my pockets,
carry to your hospital bed.

The Breezes

The sun slathers on, then grills exposed skin:
in the campos, treeless; climbing bridges, wooden,
iron, concrete, endless; on the Zattere where,
even now, at noon, Venetians stroll, walk their dogs.

We do this, even when the air is so still it sucks
inward. We do this, even when we are old, infirm, just plain fat.
We want the scenes, sounds, cobblestone truths
to marinate, bake, create a stew of memories

we can savor later, perhaps even in dementia,
when these moments may bubble up afresh from within
the deepest musculature of that part of the brain;
we may experience these vistas,

hear that plaintive gull, Veneziana din, discover thoughts
tapped while we were still in step with time;
say, or think we are saying (to the familiar face, smiling, not quite
identifiable, asking *another spoonful*

of coffee ice cream?) yes, Redentore is glorious in this light.
Why don't we stop here for lunch? It is cool, shady.
Our beloveds will translate our gibberish. Today,
I listen to gull, wake, water taxi sounds (each boat its own voice).

I cram in as much as I can: the water (green, choppy, small gull rocking,
expectant), seaweed bouquet undulating below like Ophelia;
potted geraniums, sagging with thirst; vino rosato
sipped from this tulip-shaped glass, still half full.

If nothing else, please remember, feel this breeze
fanning, stroking, at La Piscina on 9th July, 2013.
I am making memories. I capture breezes, store them,
will release them like red balloons in Alzheimer's days.

WANTING

He with blueberry eyes
hoists, then sets a table just for me
beside this slim canal.
He notes I am alone, again,
how well I look.
He sees my knees
and slender legs;
with that glance
suggests we share a drink,
one night, and now I know.

I taste *verdure griglia -*
Melanzane e zucchini.
I drizzle oil, drink wine. I want
carciofini, those tender baby artichokes,
lament the ended season.
I settle on *gnocchi Bolognese,*
cover with cheese, to please myself.

I wonder why he wants me,
the gentle, handsome man,
owner, chef,
Biennale artist,
when my season is past.
Girlish bloom and giggles
fade in family scrapbooks.
Such a surprise,
not delicious, not now,
as boats pass by.

I face the bridge, swallow *gelato* and wait
for gondolas to come.

One pokes its bow in view
and then the oar.
It never travels through,
but docks and bobs
before the ancient arch.

TIME PIECES REPAIRED

Buzzed in to her bleached blonde (teased too) domain,
I hear no ticks, no tocks, no bells, no hums.
It's close, no room to move beyond the case.
She's caged behind the glass, approaching me.
We speak above rows of old stopped watches.
I pass my slip through the cup of air there.
She seeks her surgeon's tools (no gown, no mask).

Clocks crowd the whimsy wall: clown hands, clown mask
watching me, bereft of its own domain.
A tool drops, clatters on concrete. She hums
while stooping to retrieve the spoke. The case
hides her working hands. Did she forget me?
I tap my hand against glass. She watches
me briefly, smiles, lifts a watch, my watch there.

One cuckoo clock, pillar perched. I reach there
to trace the dusted maiden's face. I mask
my move, afraid I've breached her ruled domain.
Cool china hair, paint blonde, frames lips which hum
to me, *please, place the key in my clock-case*
and turn, turn till I can dance; release me.
The sad maid stays still while no one watches.

A mirrored face reflects me. It watches
with my eyes, sliced by steel hands, still swords there.
Uncut, I step aside, jarred by my mask,
unscarred, but still I'm caught in her domain.
I stare at brown hair, parted, short; time hums
through new white strands. My mouth, briefly encased
above and left of "VI", disappoints me.

Buzz. The door quick-snaps ajar, clearing me
barely. I'm pressed against smooth cased watches.
He swerves, then lunges past me, propelled there
like thick air blasted in. His thin frame masked
with full cut suit, he fills the tight domain,
lifts his prize and, voice buzzing like bee hums,
cradles its antique mahogany case.

She glides to him, like maiden's mate, that case
their center. His arms embrace this acme,
this... clock. She grasps a side latch. He watches
as the shelf is raised to receive him. Their
breath stopped, he shifts this gift to her. No masks,
their faces flush. They rush to her domain
in back. The shelf crashes back. The shop hums.

Examining their treasure now, all hums
cease. (My watch forgotten - small, dull, gold case.)
A glance, no beat skipped, and she recalls me.
Fingers linger, then scoop my (fixed?) watch's
crystal, case, band, quick-snapped together there.
...a spring replaced. I thank her cordial mask.
The door clicks, shutting me from her domain.

On Greenwich Street, shared domain, my watch hums
on my arm. Street sounds erupt, encase me.
I watch hands there repair home. I stay masked.

COUNTING ON FRIDAY

Two dogs,
asleep on the porch.
No sun yet.
Four male mallards,
fed and gone. The runt
was hungry; three bullies
easily tricked:
the shunned one got fed
an extra slice of bread -
multigrain, bit by bit.
A noisy bunch.
Who will join me for lunch?

Unusual:
a trio of
mourning doves.
Not a fluke; last week, too.
They fly. They light. They preen.
Trio'd - not paired.
I would not want to share.

The solo rower stands
on his board, dips
his upright oar,
digs through the inland water-way.
The board tilts this way, that,
glides along, glides along.
A gentle current makes us strong.

Shade retreats.
Sparrows feast
on crumbs, left by those ducks.

The sun,
solitary,
burns through my early morning.
Coffee waits inside.
There I go, to hide.

Peeling Black

Palazzo
Above me, ceiling angels stretch, are still,
frozen just as the plump one touches Her.
Their placid faces are fixed. Crowds are slow.
I don't stop for angels' secrets. Bells peal
and fill the space where angels hover. Black
is absent in Ca' Rezzonico light.

These frescos try to enlighten me: will
I see stormy centuries, surrender
to timelessness of clouds, begin to go
beyond the dialogue of paint? I feel
the place, this Venice that cannot come back
to life, yet holds the answers to my night.

Canals
Entangled lovers get lost down the light-
filled *calles* leading over bridges. Still
waters nudge the banks, rising. Venice. Her
canals, lagoons accompany the slow
progress of others, coupled ones. Bells peal
the way to light. I choose instead the black

lacquered gondola, a serenade. Night
swells the song of the canal, saps the will
of the embrace until I surrender
passion for a tender rocking. I go
beyond the plash of oars, the tune. I feel
time drift. Drift. I drift. I turn, must come back.

Basilica Santa Maria Della Salute
Before the droning of the men in black
returns to lull the congregants, the light
plays on kneeling nuns; their faces are still
and smooth as pews. I listen: Venice. Her
voices intrude: the organ's flute, the slow
moaned prelude before the fugue. Trumpets peal.

Vespers fill the empty space, bring faith back.
One organ's orchestra rebuffs the night;
each note tugs and prods me, corrals my will.
Caught in the swollen chords, I surrender
to holy places where I rarely go.
The sound drowns me; I float in light I feel.

Hotel Excelsior
The wedding guests expect church bells to peal.
Instead, the Lido greets the groom in black
with Adriatic shores and April light.
A bride, vows and two white doves released. Still,
I miss the tolling bells. In another
month, the female dove remains. Seasons slow.

Autumn comes. The white dove huddles. She feels
the chill upon her ledge. Hotel chairs, back
inside till Spring, seat guests. We slouch in night
warmth, cashews in my mouth. Poor dove. She will
not find nuts. Her red eyes soon surrender.
She swoops to new tossed crumbs, a place to go.

Glass

Murano red is colored glass, so slow
to yield. I see the masters' hands appeal
to it, mold memory to glinting black!
It cools, stiffens. The furnace tongs of light
resurrect it. Centuries of breath still
inflate the globes, cast Virgin forms of Her.

Sequestered on Murano, secrets go
nowhere. They're shared - masters to sons. I feel
flames of regret: can't I return, turn back
when glass contained the colors of the night?
We create sprites, aventurine. We will
them to fly. Fragile, some smash, surrender.

Madonna

The courtyard wall, stones crumbling, supports Her
marbled form. Her chipped face obscures a slow
gaze. She seeks domed *Salute*. Its bells peal
all the epochs, births of popes, doges, black
plague. Palazzos sink, decay, revive. Light
returns; She listens, silent. Bells are still.

Her crown, shimmering, long since surrendered
to trinket shops, to tourists on the go.
Cement, wrought iron, wooden bridges feel
footsteps climbing, pausing, descending back.
No footprints - just the unseen dust of nights
and days, layered time, remains, come what will.

Last Bell

Will She be still? Her canals weep with Her
on stone. Slowly, Her heart begins to peal
the quarter-hour bells, peels black from light.
I ask Her. Plead. *When will you surrender?*
Go, as I have to, to an end? I feel
Her fade back. I emerge, a star, join night.

*Chapter 6: a time to seek, to lose;
to keep, to cast away.*

THE SUN IN ITS JEWEL CASE

after The Sun in Its Jewel Case, Yves Tanguy, 1937. Oil on canvas.
Peggy Guggenheim Collection, Venice, Italy

The sun is in its jewel case, vaulted.
There are bones at the dark edges
and their shadows jut

as though they were real.
Only dimness (perhaps the faintest green,
a dust of red) hints of life.

Life is gone, make no mistake.
The tease of light nudges but relents.
The artist brush skids to stop,

leaves a tinted thread.
If only I could trace the trail
beyond the cloudy canvas, perhaps

I could find a key,
turn it,
release the blue.

ELLEN B. HAS DIED ALONE

She did not flush; she did not
get her panties on -
a stick of butter on her bed
with books and toast
in jumbled sheets.

Ellen, 68,
obese again, has died.
Her eyes wide,
they stare
beyond the bed
through 137 boxes
unopened,
transfixed by the five-foot stacks
of still sealed mail -
her sentries
barring entry.

It will take eight days to breach
the barricades.
No one finds the will
she swore she wrote;
no one finds the jewelry
or safe deposit key.
No one finds the empty

space,
unhoarded,
cowered in a corner
of her smallest closet, door
ajar,
where she fed
her slender hopes.

The Importance of Telling the Tales

Thoughts of that 17th century woman of substance evaporate:
Sarra Sulam, Jew, poet who drew the brightest thinkers of her day
to her salon in the ghetto, betrayed by an amorous monk.
Giudecca bells pervade my brain -
worms through fruit.

Oh! There is the MSC Magnifica,
behemoth, inescapable at 10 stories,
followed by Norwegian Jade – I count 15 stories,
both tugged though.

When I have slept, or dined or thought more
Sarra will locate me, tug me through the deep.
She will confide from the wakes of the lagoon.

I hear, at the next table, Alabama twangs I cannot parse;
I try to stay awake
while I wait for delicious inspiration and profound branzino.

Without a Prayer

Requiem in C Minor, Luigi Cherubini

Praise to God
at Carnegie Hall tonight.

I am raised up,

my disbelief hushed
by a purr of prayer.
I do not know what spurs my
Cherubini adulation.

I am
devoid of Trinity
        Yahweh's covenants
                Allah's Mecca-seeking swarms,

yet I feel devout as any –
filled with communion rivaling Abraham's
when that ram intervened.

A small chit I – believer in nothing –
pay for this rapture:
the price of contrition
awakening tomorrow with

the musky taste
of a one-night stand.

La Lecture, Degas and My Daughter

Gallery #3, La Louvre

Renoir knew you: your hair, plump palm to mouth,
the thin slanted brows, eyes down as you read.
He drew his girls - one blonde, you red – so proud
to paint these two outside, in shades of green.
Pastoral scene, of youth, two hundred years
ago. I watch you as you reappear.

To have you here preserved so true at 9
stirs me until I pass Cezanne's steep lanes,
Monet's snowy hills. Degas' nude bath time,
opposite La Lecture, disrupts my state
of reverie, creates another clone
of you: sensual, full breasted, alone.

Slipping

I must be slipping.
I cleaned your old room today.
I flattened Ninja Turtle mountains.
I sorted through baseball boxers
you loved to pad around in
and the plaid silk ones
that made your darkness glisten.
Boxes, bags and drawers surrounded me,
your castoff snakeskins.
I wonder, under your robes,
do you now wear white?

Faltering on the middle step,
I recovered, then retrieved
(from the hollow hiding place)
a Sucrets tin
with your graffiti lid of purples, flame and orange.
I released its stale air
and pocketed your vessel.
I will hand it to you, this long-ago box,
open, ready to be filled
with your new grown treasures.

I even cleared the storage space
where we played and bumped our heads,
our cavern fun: helmets, bike rack, weights.
I tossed that past as mothers must.
I am fine
and if you are not, you have your own
room to clean.

THIS ROILING SEA

After pelting rain compelled my rescue,
I umbrella'd her, blood pressure soaring,
and fled against the gusts to her doctors.
They harbored her; they scribbled drugs of choice.
Prescriptions filled, bed made, I put her back.

Just then, the sun declared the day, beckoned
acolytes to a ray-crowned sea worship.
It deafened me, the roiling sea beyond
the dunes. I never saw such tangled crests,
boiling pots, undulating, uncoiling.

Anchored by a high moon and sun face-off,
the sky taunted the sea with unstirred blue.
At shoreline lay snakes of foam; wind-blasted
pieces dislodged, skirted sand, toppled and
disintegrated, expiating sin.

My watch announced remission's end. Enough
of deliverance for today. I trudged
through sand, pushed back the wind, pocketed hands,
reached keys and forgot to leave a healing
prayer in the wailing wall of the dunes.

At Noon, Judge Not

I might get up from this chair
and walk to the far pier at Missouri Avenue.
The waves distract me and the man walking by me
in the yellow-flowered swim trunks and white-brimmed hat -
flapping like one of the underling waves –
distracts me. 92 is the temperature
but the heat is distrait by the South Southwest winds at 15-20 miles per hour.
The sun distracts me from a still-fading moon that is a fleck in the sky's eye.

I should open the umbrella if I don't rise soon.
I count 11 people in the ocean, only 3 are children and,
I notice, the lifeguards do not appear distrait. Why do I find myself counting
as I walk, cook, sit? Perhaps I learned this as a child. Sometimes I have already
counted to 37 by the time I realize it and stop myself.
Distraught, I have wedged a jagged trough of sand under my feet
although the tide is going out so it will not fill.

Jessica Heather Has Run Aground

and everyone is looking.
Police mill inside the yellow-cordoned square of shore,
lifeguard stands on either side.
The bomb squad's come and gone I think
and she's been cleared. So, now men mount
a ladder; some scramble up her hull,
exploring her nuances. The way they're rummaging,
no one asked permission before entering.
Her rusty stern exposed
(no longer modestly submerged), she is beached -
a wild landmark - next to Caesar's Pier
at Mississippi Avenue,
usually a sleepy spot.

Where is her captain, master of motion,
bringer of disgrace?

She would have him back again, despite
this low-tide predicament. Next high tide (1:36 pm),
he could shove her back to sea
and he would stay awake this time,
guide her to those places only he has taken her
where scallops abound and fill her nets to bursting.

THE FOG

was not so thick I could not see the shells
and black sand at my feet.
I heard the sea,
felt how unsettled it was.
Who needs a clear view to walk the shoreline?

I picked a piece of seaweed,
popped its rubbery bubbles, viscous memories.
Sandpipers scurried, not so fearful they flew.
Pilings I passed whispered of when, together,
they bore the awesome weight of a grand pier,

vanished in a denser fog.

Chapter 7: a time to rend, to sew;
to be silent, to speak.

Madame Afghanistan

She sits across the aisle.
She glides her hands through azure gloves
as though no bomb fell on her neighbor's gate
yesterday.

The sand-colored hat, in close-weave straw,
seems proud to nestle her head;
the cloth tulip roots in the band
as if to say no flower must die today.

The flight attendant stows
her cane. She cannot stoop
to reach her embroidered bag,
also blue, which she refuses, politely,
to relinquish. It is stashed
between stocky calves.

She makes a trinity:
each gloved hand
and purse below,
as though summoning
a hand-sewn god
to stitch her world.

THE STAR OF DAVID

Genesis: 38

11 Judah then said to his daughter-in-law Tamar, "Live as a widow in your father's household until my son Shelah grows up."…. 13 When Tamar was told, "Your father-in-law is on his way to Timnah to shear his sheep," 14 she took off her widow's clothes, covered herself with a veil to disguise herself, and then sat down at the entrance to Enaim, which is on the road to Timnah. For she saw that, though Shelah had now grown up, she had not been given to him as his wife.

I wait for you by an olive tree, gnarled, aged,
yet its fruit - taut and smooth as young skin -
hangs in heavy bunches.
I pluck two:
stash in my
palm.

Two men of rank in long-sleeved me'il -
zizit dangling, soiled, at their calves -
pass by. Their sandals
kick sand up, sting my eyes.
My veil, affixed and still,
soothes my doubt; it has my scent
enhanced with fragrant henna and spikenard.
This veil conceals my face,
whispers a welcome -
I await you.

Widowed twice,
sent back by you to my father's house,
to sleep in a single bed,
I reject this lot

you cast for me:
barren, empty.
I shut off thoughts -
shame, even death -
remain resolved, rooted
to this spot.

You approach. I tighten the veil,
comfort my thigh with a silken screen
of deepest blue, feel my bridal sadhin
of finest linen, beneath, caressing.

Surrender your seal
Surrender your cords
Surrender your staff
to me -
these tokens of your name -
and, by this road,
with our palms pressed,
surrender.

You promise me a goat;
Ha. I have no need.
I shall be a she-goat
to destiny, with milk to nourish kings.
I reach beyond your withdrawn arms,
beyond Timnah, beyond
suckling twins beyond Judah to touch
tomorrow's sky, unveiled.
Yes, when the darkness comes,
an anointed star will shine.

What Happened?

In the well-tended park near my home,
a homeless man, gone now, sat with all his belongings.
He kept one bench for his stuff, the next for himself.
I passed by him most days.

A homeless man, gone now, sat with all his belongings
bundled in one bulging trash bag and one covered crate.
I passed by him most days.
I could never see what was inside.

Bundled in one bulging trash bag and one covered crate,
there must have been boots, blanket and a heavy coat.
Although I could never see what was inside,
he wrapped himself warmly when it snowed two winters.

There must have been more than boots, blanket and a heavy coat.
I never approached him, except once to say *please don't smoke.*
He wrapped himself warmly when it snowed two winters
in the well-tended park near my home.

CAFFE REGGIO RESERVED

A Mother
Pen in hand, she looks up. Cup empty, nose
moist, she dabs twice. The quiet tears belong
here, in the corner, where she will return
to writing this letter once he comes back
to take her order, again. Turn around.
He makes contact. Calmed, she lets her eyes close.

A Daughter
She veers to the corner table. Her long
straight saffron hair has every head turned
(she's pleased) to trace its sway below her back.
Her *Avril* looks embraced, she moves around
to face them, sits by windows, sidles close
to catch the light that glows on her trim nose.

A Husband
It's his favorite café. He returns
not often, won't sit long, but now thinks back,
from this cramped corner, to times at the round
table, years back when he and she were close.
Done, he wants to leave; she lingers. He knows
she knows. *Relax,* she says. *It won't be long.*

A Daughter
She settles in to meet her mom, leans back
on serpents: wood-carved scales and tails, rounded,
black. Fingers tap the pane. Mom. Waving, close
outside. They laugh as Mom presses her nose
and mouth on glass. Mom plays. It isn't long
before she learns her brother won't return.

A Husband (another time)
You tried so hard to turn yourself around
this last time, his absent son. Then thoughts close
down, the clawfoot, marble-topped table no
support for the father's restless longing
for this banished child. Cornered, he returns
to stirring jasmine tea. The spoon's placed back.

A Mother
Absently, her fingers open and close
around jaw armrests clamped on rubbed, unknown
prey. What else? *Do good. Try! It won't be long*
if you stay clean.? Don't preach. Instead, she turns
to the check, pockets the pen, pushes back
and surrenders her son to his next round.

Reserved sign's gone, no longings left. They turn
off lights each night. Chairs are back under round
and corner tables. The Reggio's closed.

HALLELU

for Rabbi Sharon Kleinbaum
after protest of Congregation Beit Simchat Torah by the
Westboro Baptist Church, June 21, 2009

A boy stood, back to the Hudson,
a noose around his neck.
Young, 9 or so, he hugged his heavy sign,
fingers cramped with the fervor
of clenching each side of this sign
that clung to him and hung him
as he watched, unflinching.
Bitchburger, it said, in thick bold black
atop a baby in a bun. *Hold it high, young man!*

Hang it high, my son! Look devils in the eye.
The big man, 10 signs tall,
loomed near, rooted to the gravel
that may bear the corpse of his son's soul
if it comes thrashing down,
as it may,
strangled by cords of hate.

We flow behind her, *Hallelu,*
her rainbow trident held aloft,
toward the Hudson, *Haleluhu,*
the banter unheard, *Haleluhu,*
beyond the barricade.
The song of Psalm 150 pours from us like tears,
soaks the ground, *Haleluhu,*
and grows a tallit tree that spreads its branches
wide enough, like hers, to shelter us
from these slurs.

We face hate, *Haleluhu,*
with her clear, undaunted eyes.
One of us leans in and whispers
What is a Bitchburger?
I shrug, as our reprise resonates, *Haleluhu,*
in a sapphire sky. *Halleluyah.*

A Cappella

The song bird woke me, 5:10 am today.
He has done so all of May -
a cappella, perfect pitch,
close by. I cannot see his perch,

cannot translate his lyrics.
I feel his joy pronounced, rich
in aria. Clear sky or rain,
his hope revives each day.

By 5:20, he has soared
to a farther stage. I strain to hear
the fading trills. No more.
Sometimes he returns; encore.

The morning curtain's drawn:
Carmeni bells ring six gongs;
the boats and gulls first moan;
the soloist has flown.

A New Day

In Memory of Syril and Herb Dratfield, z"l

Before the others
wake, she and he bustle
- as only 90 or so years can -
in slippers over the oak floor,
greet me as though I, waiting
with the clothed table, mug in hand,
were their flesh and blood,
favored with the low
voice at dawn,
first to wake,
first to take
a slowly turned word
or two, meant just for me,
as though - if quietly and carefully spoken -
the sentence would never end.

Chapter 8: a time to love, to hate;
a time for war, for peace.

LANDBOUND

Perhaps water wedding vows last longer
than inland nuptials. Perhaps the stronger
tides forge fiercer bonds. Blessings - preachers shout
above the sea swell sounds, so high, so loud
they must be heeded. Sequined bodice folds
of those brides heave in synch with seagull squalls,
shimmer prismatic drops, like ocean spray,
dazzle grooms to love for eternity.

Venetian brides hold tight to rosaries,
en route to Chiesa dei Carmini,
cross canals that course veinlike through their hearts.
The Catholic bells and *till death do us part*
fuse with water taxi hums and soft wakes
against campo stone walls, as each groom takes
a bride, exchanges rings, and those close know
that love resides within the Lagoon's glow.

I doubt that studies have been done. Who cares
but me? Perverse theory, unkind, unfair
in view of landbound lovers' plights: inside
dining clubs, muralled walls, candescent light,
or worse. Just vows, white gowns and smashing glass.
Can love last, without waves and crashing crests,
cemented far from lakes, creeks, Jersey shores,
with one kiss, ours, sealing forever?

BITE

Shoah Memorial

This soldier's glee stuns me
all these years later.
I hope he died at war, in combat or as captive,
defeated, his smile erased.
There is no solace for the Jew, frail, bearded,
at his feet, tripped or booted, petrified
by the stones of death he sensed
as he wore the dusty shroud of this road.
Surely both are dead.

I can't erase a Nazi smile,
more than the eyes of two-year old Hannah Greenberg,
the other one million plus five-hundred thousand lights
of Shoah children, lost,
more than the five ceramic bells dressing the young Jew,
weighing down her small chest with stars of David,
still brown eyes asking what next.

Even teeth bite full-throttle youth,
in this faded photo, sixty years ago,
gnaw weeks after I am safely home.
This grin raves still,
repeats past eyes, lives in chests and feet,
like terror against my raised hand.

Victoria

Brandenberg Gate

I saw her face last night
when all had fled
to schnitzels, wursts and bed:
tilted,
eyes cast left
in midnight's glare.
Unmoved, she did not blink.

Then morning came.
Awake, she arched
her winged back,
gripped tighter her trident,
and listened, unrequited,
for the stomping surge,
the thrilling march
of victorious troops.

Bikes scooted through
her famous gate.
Joggers passed
as gawkers trickled in,
busloads soon to join.

She waits.
Tulips are tended.

FURLED AT BRANDENBURG GATE

He crouches close to tulips,
camera fixed, clicked.
They watch him,
intent, oblivious to them -
she, the wife from Jersey,
beside in baggy tourist tee, and
she, Victoria, crowned above -
both reprieved by his
indifference,
his devotion to a plant.

Her reins slack,
the prancing steeds
need no command
to lead her chariot
always onward.
What matters where?
To France and back?
To annihilation of the Jews,
to Teaneck?

Her wings unclipped,
poised, she does not
unfurl and fly.
Inside the bucket
in which Victory rides
hide tokens of our plight,
unseen by gazers
just off the bus
who glance up, but then
forget
we, too, have glimpsed
weariness,
wasted might.

Il Trenino

The little train to Cividale,
three cars long,
second class only,
starts with *peep-peep.*
One of three in our car
says *choo-choo.*
I cannot see him smile
but I do. The big train
from Santa Lucia Venezia
to Udine, sounded loud
heartbeats, massive,
like a man,
slow to start, each bass beat
round, full,
one - *chug* -
pause
one - *chug* -
pause,
then gained speed
chug chug chug-chug chug-chug-chug-chug
till it raced to a palpitating whir.
The little train purrs like a Lionel
with intermittent tweets of horn,
like my brother Michael's set,
with rambling track and just
two stops.

In our recreation room,
in our pajamas, we played,
built tracks, connected them
until the trains tooted to the stations.
Dad lent Mike's set to Cousin Tom -
like so much else to come - pieces lost:
Dad, Tom and the train set he kept.
Those Lionels *peep-peeped* like this,

purred on pitch like this,
crowded out thoughts,
other sounds –
upstairs screams, something thrown, sobs –
kept us kids at peace.

We slow. We stop at Moimaco,
where most have never been
and will not ever go.
The windows fog,
hide the last stop.
peep peep peep
announces our end.

I step quickly off the platform
to begin,
in this ancient land of Lombards,
something new.

New Boards

They've dismantled the pier -
where you proposed
forty years ago -
restoring piling
by rotting piling
of this once fine fishing pier.

This crisp March day,
abundant sun,
is so unlike that day:
August goose-bump rain.
Eyes reddened by Dad's mean turn,
I leaned on boardwalk rails

and sifted words from wakes.
I sorted tears and rain,
eyes fixed on the pier.
You grabbed my hand.
You yanked me right, down steps,
under pier boards.

Umbrellas of Cherbourg
comes to mind now.
Not then. I saw crests and
tented pilings, ushers to the sea,
under that wooden chuppah,
ringed by your arms. You asked.

They've ripped off the top
and fresh beige beams,
firmly fixed, hold promise.
The spot where we once stood
will fit kids only. In late Fall,
let's walk across the new boards.

About the Author

Sherri Felt Dratfield graduated from Goucher College and is a member of the Phi Beta Kappa Society. She received an M.F.A. in Acting from the University of Denver and holds a J.D., with election to Order of the Coif, from New York University School of Law. Sherri is the author of two previous collections of poetry, *The City* (Finishing Line Press, 2013) and *Water Vigils* (Finishing Line Press, 2014). Both collections were nominated for a Pushcart Prize. Her poems have appeared in various journals and anthologies and have been awarded recognition in the Margaret Reid Contest for Traditional Verse, Jewish Currents' Raines Poetry Competition and the Passager Poetry Contest. Sherri lives in the West Village of Manhattan with her husband, Simon. They visit their shore home in Ventnor City, New Jersey during all seasons.

www.ingramcontent.com/pod-product-compliance
Lightning Source LLC
Chambersburg PA
CBHW022157080426
42734CB00006B/467